Pent Up Thoughts

Pent Up Thoughts

James B. Agape

Published by James B. Agape, 2024.

While every precaution has been taken in the preparation of this book, the publisher assumes no responsibility for errors or omissions, or for damages resulting from the use of the information contained herein.

PENT UP THOUGHTS

First edition. April 3, 2024.

Copyright © 2024 James B. Agape.

ISBN: 979-8224405619

Written by James B. Agape.

Table of Contents

I dedicate this book to my beloved mother, who sacrificed everything she had to give me a better life.Our lives haven't been easy, but we've weathered the high seas together and can at least take a breather from the rocky waters that have always seemed to wreak havoc in our lives.

Please, when you read this book, don't feel disheartened by the inner conflicts it portrays. At the time, I had pushed everyone away and decided to keep my pain to myself.

Rather, smile, for I have come a long way, and I am much better than I was then.

Journaled Thoughts, Messages, and Poems By: James B. Agape

"Whispers of Restless Shadows"

This section basically delves into the winding nature of anxiety and depression, capturing my raw emotions and struggles of living with these conditions. It offers a nuanced portrayal of my inner battles and the weight of invisible burdens that I often have to endure on a daily basis.

Recovery is not a straight line, but every setback is a lesson in resilience. Keep going, keep growing, and keep fighting for the life you deserve.

Believe you're worthy of existing.

Living with anxiety or depression,
Can make life seem like a huge confusion.
It's like walking on a tightrope,
Always feeling like you might just lose hope.
The challenges can seem insurmountable,
The pain and fear almost unbearable.
But with each step you take,
You build resilience and strength to move forward.
There are days you'll feel like you're drowning,
But reaching out is better than frowning.
Talking to someone can ease the weight,
And help you see there is still hope to create.
With each sunrise is a new story to write,
A chance to embrace the light.
The struggles you face are part of your journey,
But with resilience, you'll find your victory.
The triumphs may be small,
But each one is a step toward a win.
Managing anxiety or depression,
Is not easy, but with time you'll find a new expression.
Don't give up or feel like you're alone,
You're not and the seeds of hope are sown.
With each step, you take a victory you gain,
And before long, the strength of your will reigns.

There are times when I cling to happiness, and like a shot of whiskey, I consume it and feel its intensity within my heart and depraved soul in its entirety, and like waking from a dream, I awaken to my weary reality that's riddled with sadness, pain, and emptiness. I can't escape it, and so I try to manage my unhinged thoughts, which for the most part drive me insane only because I'm aware that reality is constant and inescapable.

Anxiety, a constant companion by my side,
Telling me I'll never be enough, no matter how much I try.
Depression, a heavy cloud above my head,
Whispering that I'm better off staying in bed.

A constant battle rages within,
A storm that rages without end.
Anxiety and depression, my lifelong foe,
Always lurking, always near, never letting go.
My mind, a battlefield fraught with doubt,
Invisible chains holding me down, pulling me about.
Every breath is a struggle, every thought a fight,
A long and arduous journey into the night.
But amidst the darkness, a flicker of light,
A guiding star shining through the gloom.
A glimmer of hope, a glint of steel,
The power within to conquer all that I feel.

Taking care of your mental health isn't a luxury; it's a priority. A necessity, if you will. Don't wait until you're struggling to prioritize your well-being. Although I might say that there are days when I indulge myself in work until late into the night to avoid what I'm feeling inside, sadly, it's only a partial remedy because my thoughts are always with me, ever present, never relinquishing their thirst for tormenting me.

The weight of the world rests heavy on my chest
Every breath is a struggle, a constant test
Anxiety grips me, a vice around my throat
Depression lingers, a storm cloud that won't float
I try to shake it off, to find some peace
But these demons within won't seem to cease
They follow me everywhere, day and night
A haunting presence that won't take flight
I put on a brave face, a smile to disguise
The turmoil raging beneath my eyes
But the facade cracks and I feel exposed
All the pain, the fear, now fully disclosed

Living with anxiety or depression,
Is like being trapped in a never-ending dimension.
Every day is filled with fear,
And the struggle is always nearby.
It's like a storm that brews within,
A whirlwind of emotions that's hard to win.
But with each step, I take a leap of faith,
Hoping to find a way out of this scary space.
I yearn to break away and savor life,
To bask in all the pleasures that make my soul thrive.
But I know it's a voyage that takes time,
Thus, I shall not give up hope and keep pushing on, divine.
With loved ones and kindred spirits by my side,
And the fortitude that I keep in me, deep inside,
I'll keep gleaming like a star, oh so bright,
Through every hurdle that I overcome with might.
If you feel lost and alone,
Just remember that you aren't by yourself.
You have the strength to keep on fighting,
And soon, you'll overcome this struggle, and everything will be
alright again.

To this day, I get so antsy and anxious at the thought of opening WhatsApp, Gmail, and Instagram. To the point where I have more or less done away with WhatsApp and my family and friends have to call to reach me. Don't get me started with emails. You never quite know what to expect, and it gives me this sinking feeling in my stomach. Similar to Instagram, although it's a necessary evil if I'm ever going to get my thoughts out into the world.

In the depths of despair,
I wander a lonely road,
A heart full of sorrow,
A soul that can't be consoled.
My mind, a battlefield,
Torn and scarred by worry,
Anxiety my constant companion,
A burden that I must carry.
The weight of depression,
Heavy upon my heart,
Its grip, unrelenting,
Tears my world apart.
But still, I soldier on,
Through the darkness and the pain,
For I know that hope still exists,
That sunshine follows the rain.
And though my path is difficult,
And the struggles never cease,
I find comfort in knowing,
With each step I increase,
My strength, my resilience,
My ability to keep fighting,
Until the darkness fades,
And the light of hope is shining.

Managing anxiety and depression is not a battle to be won, but a journey to be embraced. The triumph is in the progress made, no matter how small.

Each morning, I wake with a weight on my chest,
My heart racing, and my mind unable to rest.
The world feels like an overwhelming space,
And my thoughts race at an unrelenting pace.
The past creeps in with memories I dread,
And the future looms with worries in my head.
It's like a shadow that refuses to fade away,
And I struggle to visualize the light of day.
Sometimes I feel like I'm stuck in a pit,
With no escape from this endless darkness.
But I remind myself to hold on tight,
To keep fighting through the darkest of nights.
I inhale a deep breath and face my fears,
Drying anxious tears with gentle care.
Each day feels like an arduous battle, it's clear,
But I refuse to let it defeat me, I'll fight and soldier on.
I'm confident I'll find my way, one day
And break free from anxiety's endless fray.
Until then, I'll keep fighting strong,
And pray for a day when I'm finally free from this lifelong song.

Self-care isn't selfish; it's self-preservation. Prioritizing your mental health means being kind to yourself, and that's something you deserve. Don't be in a rush. Vibe alone if you have to until you come back to yourself.

In the depths of darkness, I find myself
Trapped in a world of endless pain
A constant struggle to keep from falling
The weight of it all driving me insane
Anxiety grips me, its claws sharp and cold
Whispers of doubt fill my mind
The fear of failure, of being alone
A prison that's hard to unwind
Depression creeps in like a thief in the night
Stealing my joy, my hope and my light
It whispers lies and feeds on my fears
Leaving me lost, drowning in tears
Clasping onto Hope's delicate strand,
A flicker of radiance in the night,
I am not alone in this demand,
Together, we can keep hope alight.
I'll fight to keep on moving,
To take each step with intention,
Even when life feels like it's bruising,
I know I can find redemption.

I remember days when I used to be quite talkative, happy, and quick-witted. Then, as if someone flipped a switch, my persona changed when life happened. I got quieter, indifferent, and colder, and I couldn't smile as often.

In my head, I feel the weight
of anxiety that won't abate
Simple tasks are hard to start
And my mind and body drift apart
The world around me starts to shrink
As my thoughts move fast and think
I feel alone, I feel so small
As anxiety takes over all
But I know I am not alone
Many others have felt this tone
With help and guidance, we can see
The future bright and anxiety-free
With strength, we face each day
And slowly, doubts will melt away
There will be struggles, I won't pretend
But with hope, our journey won't end
Triumphs come in small and big
Every victory, a chance to dig
Deep down and find the grit we need
To keep on moving, to succeed
Let's raise a glass to us
To the ones who fight with every thrust
Against anxiety and depression's grip
We'll come out strong, we won't slip.

My overbearing mind has dug its claws deep within me. I struggle to sleep every night. Hell, I'm tired of acting like I'm alright, yet I aspire to see the sunrise.

In the depths of my mind, twists and turns,
Anxiety and depression, my heart yearns.
Challenges await me at every turn,
But somehow, I must learn.
Sadness wraps its arms around me,
Causing my soul to be weary,
But somehow, I push through,
With every victory, my soul renews.
I manage the demons within,
With each step, I refuse to give in,
For I know there is a light at the end,
And I must endeavour to transcend.
Through the trials, I will find my way,
With every breath, I find the strength to stay,
I will triumph over every doubt and fear,
And in the end, my soul will cheer.
In the face of anxiety and depression,
I have found my way to redemption,
And with every challenge I overcome,
I am stronger!

Living with depression and anxiety can feel like being stuck in a storm. But remember, storms always pass, and the sun will shine again.

Anxiety and depression, they're not just words,
But feelings that can shake you to the core.
They're battles fought inside, not with swords,
With days that seem endless, leaving you sore.
You wake up and the world feels like a haze,
A fog that envelops your every thought.
The weight on your chest threatens to daze you,
And the fear inside, it can't be fought.
But amidst the gloom, there's a ray of light,
A spark of hope that helps you fight.
If you hold on, with all your might,
You'll find that things can turn out right.
It may not be easy, but never give in,
Every step forward is a win.
Each day you manage, that's a triumph,
A sign that you're stronger than you think.
Anxiety and depression, may lead,
But you have the power to take the lead.
The challenges may be tough, that's true,
But remember, you have the strength to break through.

The darkness of anxiety and depression can make it hard to see the light, but remember that it's always there. You just need to keep moving forward to find it.

At some point, I tried alcohol because I thought it would help me numb my pain. I just wanted something that would make me mellow and help ease my mental anguish. Boy, was I wrong? All it did was escalate my misery. As a matter of fact, I'd end up sobbing myself to sleep. It's as if the liquor made my pain, suffering, and depression palpable. Don't even consider the "devil's drink" as a remedy. It'll just add to your problems... Trust me, I have been there and done that.

I'm at a point where I am not sure whether I am depressed or just numb inside. Because here's the thing: Nothing excites or captivates me anymore. Not movies, concerts, or hangouts. I'm just there. I feel nothing; I'm neither sad nor happy. I'm empty; that's how I feel. However, I'm thankful for books, music, and coffee. For now, all I can do is lose myself in books. Occasionally, I let my emotions bleed and permeate through paper. It's keeping me going. At least I have peace of mind.
The Depth of My Emptiness

All I can pray and hope for is that one day I'll get to see the light, and it will act like a beacon to help me crawl out of this sunken abyss that I've found myself in. I'm confident it's bound to happen because lately I've been dreaming of paradise. Perhaps it's a sign of what's to come.

The weight of the world on my shoulders,
Anxiety and depression, constant tormentors,
A battle within, every single moment,
An unending struggle, a constant opponent.
But I found strength within myself,
I learned to embrace my pain and delve,
Into the depths of my broken mind,
To discover the fragments left behind.
I learned to breathe, to let go,
To take control and let my inner strength grow,
To see the beauty in small victories,
And appreciate each moment, without worries.
Each sunrise, each breath, a triumph,
Each moment of peace, an achievement,
I overcame the demons within,
And found the light that had been dim.
Now I stand tall, my head held high,
With a heart full of hope and the courage to fly,
I am a warrior, a survivor, a conqueror,
Of anxiety and depression, forever more.

Worry and anxiety can drive you into a state of paralysis. I, for one, have experienced such, and I have figured it's best to face situations that drive up my anxiety head-on. That way, I don't give my thoughts an opportunity to talk me out of taking action. When I am worried, I try to focus on the present. Worry creeps up when we are constantly thinking about future outcomes. Live in the now and focus on getting through today. Regaining power and control from the overlords of worry and anxiety.

Beneath the weight of anxious thoughts,
A heavy burden takes its toll,
Uncertainty grips the heart and soul,
And every day becomes a fight.
But Hope still whispers in your ear,
And Courage nudges from within,
With every breath, a new beginning,
And every step, a chance to win.
Take heart, dear one, and know,
That though the road is dark and steep,
With each small victory, you show,
Your demons' power starts to sleep.
For in the valleys of our fears,
We find a seed that's yet to grow,
A strength that will last for years,
And a light that will always glow.
And though the road ahead is fraught,
The love and grace that you possess,
Will be your armor, your support,
And in the end will bring success.

These days, you might bump into long-time friends, old acquaintances, or just casual acquaintances and schedule a catch-up session, but the disappointing thing is that the conversations are shallow and surface-level. superficial, if you will. Where do you work now? Which neighborhood do you live in? How much money do you make? Are you driving? Oh, really, which make and model? I find it shallow. Few are those who dare ask whether you're happy and how you're faring mentally and spiritually. What's the point of accumulating all the materialism and riches this world has to offer if you're still unhappy inside? Certainly, I understand that it makes life easier and whatnot. However, I think having genuine and deep conversations goes a long way toward forming better human connections. It's refreshing.

Through days of darkness and despair,
With thoughts and worries beyond repair,
Remember, dear friend, that hope is there,
And love can heal and show you care.
The burden of anxiety may grow immense,
Yet despair not, for hope shall be your defence,
Each moment gifts an opportunity to mend,
And joy, not far off, awaits your brave transcend.
Take a step, gentle and slow,
Inhale deeply, let the air bestow,
There's boundless joy, both near and far,
Just open your eyes, see the wonders as they are.
The road to recovery may not be simple or plain,
But each victory, no matter how small, is never in vain,
And the love and support around you will remain,
Guiding you towards a brighter, happier domain.
Hold on, dear friend, and don't let worry reign,
Seek help and never let anxiety or depression detain you,
For there is always a way to break the chain,
And let positivity and happiness into your life again.

In the depths of despair,
When life's burdens seem unfair,
And darkness shadows every step,
Encouragement is what we seek to get.
To us, it may seem bleak and tiresome,
As if every hope and dream has expired,
But know that there's power in persistence,
And strength in facing our resistance.
Beloved, don't let burdens on your shoulders press too deep,
Each breath and prayer can transform the darkness that seeps.
Take each stride gently, dear beating heart of mine,
Discover the hope that eternally does shine.
Encouragement is a beacon of light,
Guiding you through even the darkest night.
Lift your head, my precious friend,
And know that hope will never end.

You are not alone in your struggles. You are loved, you are valuable, and you have the strength within you to overcome your challenges. I always admire the sheer will and grit of the buffalo in the Savannah. They're always striving for their right to exist in this world, even in the face of their sworn arch enemies, the Lions. They never fold, nor do they go down without a fight.

"Blossoming into One's Self"

Celebrating self-love and self-acceptance, this section is meant to empower you to embrace your vulnerabilities, quirks, and imperfections. The poems, messages, and thoughts shed light on the beauty of authenticity, encouraging people to find strength and acceptance in their unique journeys.

Embracing your imperfections and vulnerabilities is a sign of true strength. It takes courage to show up as your authentic self and love yourself unconditionally. Only you can fill that empty void of love and acceptance that you constantly crave.

In a world that tries to change us,
It's easy to get lost and feel helpless,
But in moving forward, we must first start
By looking deep within our own hearts.
For there, we'll find a shining light,
A flame that burns both day and night,
A gentle voice that whispers soft,
Reminding us that we're enough.
We're here to love and be loved too,
To unlock the power that lies within you,
To walk with grace and confidence,
And to embrace our imperfections with resilience.
Let us celebrate ourselves today,
In every single little way,
With hugs, kind words, self-care,
And with poetry that reminds us we're rare.
For we are all unique and one-of-a-kind,
Each of us is a masterpiece waiting to shine,
Let's be proud of who we are,
And spread love and joy both near and far.

You are good enough.
You are smart enough.
You are strong enough.
You are courageous enough.
You are beautiful enough.
You are generous enough.
and you'll always be; believe it to be true, and let no one tell you otherwise.

It's been a long self-love and acceptance journey, but you have finally become grounded. You have found yourself and determined your worth. As a result, some within your social circles might think that you have become selfish. The truth is, you have become harder to manipulate. Don't confuse the two.

I want you to commit today to never speak to yourself in a manner you wouldn't speak to a friend or confidant. Begin talking to yourself the way a supportive parent, friend, or teacher would. "_Refrain from negative self-talk as much as possible_." Otherwise, your subconscious mind will perceive it as true, and this will form the basis for your life.

There are days when I have the zeal for life, the earnest yearn to relish every moment, but quite often these days I'm merely a human shell gliding through the motions of life.

I am enough, just as I am
No longer will I give a damn
About the lies that I've been told
I am beautiful, strong, and bold
I won't try to fit into society's mold,
No more pressure to do as I'm told.
Living my life true to myself,
Being who I am and nobody else.
No more doubts, no more hate,
Rejecting a life predetermined by fate.
Celebrating my unique style,
Embracing my true self with a genuine smile.

I don't know who needs to hear this, but your inability to deal with your insecurities is making you project a lot when you are mingling and interacting with people.

When you gaze into the mirror, what do you see?
A reflection of yourself or something else entirely?
Are those eyes looking back at you filled with joy or pain?
Do you see love or hate, sunshine or rain?
If your reflection shows imperfections and flaws,
Remember, it's all part of life's natural cause.
You are unique and one-of-a-kind,
So, celebrate yourself and leave the negativity behind.
Love yourself, accept who you are,
And your life will soar and reach the stars.
When you cherish the person that you see,
You'll find inner peace and feel truly free.
When you stand before the mirror,
Speak kindly to yourself, and show yourself love so pure.
Embrace your flaws and every imperfection,
For they make you unique, a perfect reflection of your
creation.

You are unique and one-of-a kind. Celebrate your quirks and flaws because they make you who you are, and that is something to be proud of.

Let us bask in the embrace,
Of love and self-acceptance's grace,
For within us lies the key,
To live a life that's positively free.
Our bodies may be different
But we are all significant
Celebrate your unique traits
And appreciate your fate
Speak kindly to yourself
And place your doubts on a shelf
Forgive your mistakes
And give yourself some breaks
Life is too short to live in disdain
So let your self-love reign
Embrace your feelings and thoughts
And cherish what you've got
Now's the moment to rejoice,
With unbridled joy, let your voice resound,
For you, my dear, are extraordinary,
Embrace your worth, let self-love be found.

Ladies, you don't need to "fix" your looks. You don't need another creme, serum, or foundation. You don't need fillers or Botox. You don't need surgery. You look normal, and you look pretty the way you are now. You're beautiful. You're special and magnificent.

In the quiet of the night
When the world seems out of sight
The stars above shine bright
I am learning to love my light
For so long, I sought to please
Others and their wishes and needs
But now I see, it's time to seize
The chance to love and be at ease
My flaws and quirks are what make me
Unique, beautiful, and who I'm meant to be
It's time to set myself free
And embrace my true identity
Let's all celebrate self-love and self-acceptance
For it is the key to true happiness and balance
Let us not judge or seek constant reassurance
Let us love ourselves, with all our imperfections.

It's fulfilling to receive validation and attention from outsiders because it reaffirms what we already believe to be true about ourselves. However, don't let it become an addiction. Especially with the blossoming of social media platforms like Instagram and TikTok. Attention and validation can be one hell of a drug, and if you aren't careful, they'll never be enough. You might spiral down the path to a dark abyss of doing anything and everything under the sun, all in the name of getting that sweet dopamine hit of attention and external validation. Always remember to keep yourself in check. Don't let it get to your head, alright?

We are all beautiful, meticulously put together and molded by The Potter, the one who beholds the heavens and sets in place the stars and the moon so that we may gaze and reflect upon the greatness of his glory, majesty, and splendor, the ruler of all nations and the one who can change the course of a king's heart like the waters of a stream, yet you shimmer at the thought of setting foot outside for fear of not measuring up to society's standards.

Don't you see? You're as free as the winds of the high seas, which blow in whichever direction they please. Cast aside the doubts mangled in your mind, spread your wings, and soar on high like the eagle, for you are made in Christ's image and likeness.

Don't let your self-love and self-acceptance journey turn you into a self-absorbed and narcissistic human being.

Embrace your imperfections,
As they make you unique.
Don't hide behind a mask,
Allow your true self to speak.
Vulnerability is power,
Not something to be ashamed.
For every flaw and weakness,
Bring forth a strength untamed.
Embrace your inner voice,
Let it speak loud and clear.
For it is with imperfection,
Our true selves come near.
The world may judge and criticize,
But know you are enough.
Allow yourself to be imperfect,
And life will surely be tough.
But with every stumble and fall,
You'll find the strength to rise.
Embrace your imperfections,
For they're a gift in disguise.

Self-love isn't just about achieving perfection (*no one is perfect; perfection is unattainable*); it's about embracing yourself with all your flaws and realizing that you are deserving of love and a sense of belonging.

Beloved, don't fret over your flaws,
They're what make you beautifully raw.
Your imperfections are a work of art,
A masterpiece of a beating heart.
Take off the mask of perfection, my dear,
Show the world your truth, let it appear.
Vulnerability is where the strength lies,
And it takes courage to unveil your disguise.
Let your scars be the story,
Of all the battles you've fought and won, in all their glory.
It makes you stronger, more resilient and wiser,
A force to be reckoned with, amazing in everyone's eyes.
Let go of your inhibitions,
Embrace your imperfections with all your convictions.
You'll find your greatest gifts lie within,
And that's where true happiness begins.

Forget about the beauty standards set by the dominant media. And just because you can't live up to those standards doesn't make you a lesser human. Through my lenses, you are not only beautiful and well put together, but your gentle spirit and soft heart breed in me a concoction of jealousy masked in admiration. You are like a priceless antique—unique and one in a million. Stop discounting yourself. Walk with your head held high and give yourself credit because you owe that much to yourself.

I don't know who needs to hear this, but if you're average, that's okay. Most people are average, and even those who are above average have their insecurities. Don't get lost comparing yourself to people who took a gazillion pictures with the perfect lighting from the perfect angle and then edited and added a bunch of filters to those pictures. Always remember that you are fearfully and wonderfully made. **Psalms 139.**

In life, we strive for perfection,
But the reality is a different direction.
Embrace the flaws, the quirks, the scars,
For they make you unique among the stars.
The world may try to make you hide,
But don't be afraid to show your inside.
It takes courage to be vulnerable,
And in that strength lies power immeasurable.
In your imperfections, you'll find beauty,
A shining light that shines truly.
Stand tall, be proud of who you are,
For your uniqueness is your shining star.

In embracing imperfections lies true power,
A strength that's felt in every shattered hour.
For in our faults, we find our shared humanity,
And in our vulnerability, we find our divinity.
The world may tell us we must be perfect and strong,
But in our weaknesses, we find where we belong.
It takes true courage to show our scars,
To open up and reveal our hearts.
For it is in our brokenness that we can learn to mend,
And in our vulnerability, we find our true friends.
Thus, let us embrace our flaws, our quirks, our fears,
And find the beauty that lies within our tears.
For it is in embracing imperfections that we can truly shine,
And in our vulnerability, we find a divine strength.
Let's not be ashamed of the things that make us real,
For it is in our imperfections that we find our greatest seal.

True beauty lies in embracing your imperfections and owning your vulnerabilities. Love your body and take care of it. Cultivate a habit of eating high-vibrational foods like fruits and veggies (don't forget meat), and hydrate. Occasionally, discipline your body by practicing intermittent fasting. Also, make sure your mind is a safe space by cultivating the habits of mindfulness and meditation.

In moments of weakness, we often feel lost
Our guard is down and we pay the price
But vulnerability can be a gift in disguise
For in it, we may uncover our inner prize
It takes great courage to let down our guard
To reveal our fears and break down our walls
But in this act, we become incredibly strong
For we realize our resilience has been there all along
It's not a weakness to admit we're not okay
It's an act of bravery, to let the world see us this way
And those who truly care will stand by our side
Encouraging us to keep going, to take it in stride
Don't be afraid to show your vulnerable side
In it, you may just find the strength you've been trying to hide
True strength comes not from walls built high
But from embracing our truth and letting our vulnerability fly.

In moments when we fall apart,
With tears streaming and a trembling heart,
We find the strength we need to start,
By tapping into our vulnerable part.
Our weaknesses may seem like flaws,
But they can be our greatest cause,
To grow and heal, to break free of laws,
And find the power within our paws.
Vulnerability is where we find,
The courage to face and not mind,
Our fears, doubts and worries that bind us;
And transcend them to be redefined.
Don't be afraid of showing true,
Emotions that make you feel so blue,
For in them lies the strength anew,
To be more than you ever knew.
Embrace your tender heart, take flight,
Witness yourself soar to new heights,
In life, exude a gentle might,
From the bravery you nurtured, igniting light.

It's there; I feel its depth, the sorrow, the pain, and the tribulations harbored in me. Yet, at this moment, I can't seem to shed tears anymore. I wish to the heavens that I would, you know, just ease off all this pressure bearing down on me and let it all out.

Read books, listen to music, visit art galleries, spend time in nature, smell flowers, visit coffee shops in different towns and cities, and spend time in museums. Stroll to the beach and enjoy the soft white sand as you soak in the sun and admire the aesthetic nature of the universe. These are some of the steps to re-design your soul and decorate your life. This is how you mark the beginning of your self-love journey. And no, you don't need to do all these activities with friends; some paths you have to tread alone. So, don't be opposed to the idea of spending time alone as you engage in the aforementioned activities. After all, it's for your benefit. Your future self will thank you.

In a world that demands strength,
I tried to hide my flaws,
But life had other plans,
And it shook me to the core.
I had to face my demons,
And confront my deepest fears,
Only then did I begin to understand,
The power of my tears.
For in letting go of my guard,
I found a newfound peace,
And though it was a scary leap,
It brought me a sweet release.

There's strength in vulnerability. Don't be afraid to show your true self to the world, because your authenticity and vulnerability inspire others to do the same.

Men are tough, strong and brave,
That's what we're often led to believe,
But beneath those masks of masculinity,
Lies vulnerability and subtlety.
Society tells us it's weak to show emotion,
To wear our hearts on our sleeves, a notion,
But it's time to break the stigma and be true,
To admit that, yes, we have feelings too.
It takes immense courage to be vulnerable,
To show our soft sides, to be approachable,
To open up and share our fears and doubts,
To take off the armor that surrounds.
Let's stand together, break down the walls,
Let's embrace our emotions, no matter how small,
Because when we're honest, we break the chains,
And that's when true strength and growth we'll gain.
Yes, men can be vulnerable, and that's okay,
It's time to celebrate it, and pave the way,
For a world where emotions are honored and seen,
And men can be themselves, whole and serene.

I'd be lying if I said I knew how to be vulnerable. Unfortunately, I've been betrayed a couple of times before, and as a countermeasure, I have built walls. A hard shell, if you will. I hardly let anyone in anymore. You see, I fear revealing my struggles and how I feel because I've done it before, and it's been used against me. It takes a great deal of effort for me to let my guard down and express my feelings. Those who've interacted with me can attest to it.

Also, the fact that society has this notion about men being stoic and immovable hasn't helped my case. So, what do I do? I keep it inside, bottled up, for fear of being ostracized by my fellow brethren. I know you think that's immature or toxic, and honestly, I can't blame you. The upside is that I've learned how to better manage my emotions. I don't let things get the best of me. I stay calm and composed, or maybe I'm making up excuses for not taking considerable action toward breaking down my erect walls.

I've been in situations where what I disclosed to confidants in private has been disclosed to others... Do you have any idea what that does to a person or how embarrassing it is? All that trust and respect went on a whim, just because someone wanted to be the center of attention. I guess loose lips sink ships, and perhaps I am partly to blame for my lack of discernment when vetting people. The good news is that I'm learning to observe people's mannerisms so that I can learn their character before opening up or being vulnerable. Talk about being accountable.

It's uncomfortable being vulnerable or opening up. Certainly, it's caused me to lose a relationship or two. (Deal with your trauma, folks.) I guess we've all got to trust somebody at some point, right?

Men can be vulnerable,
though society says it's a flaw,
the pressure to be strong and stoic
often leaves them on the wrong side of the law.
Tears are viewed as a weakness,
and so, they are often kept at bay,
but suppressing emotions can lead to
a tumultuous path on life's way.
It's time to dismantle the stereotype,
that man must always be tough,
to ask for help is not a crime,
and it's okay to feel rough.
Men have hearts that can shatter,
and minds that can overflow,
they too deserve support and care,
emotional health, a right they should know.

You are not defined by your mistakes, your past, or your flaws. You are a unique and beautiful work in progress, worthy of love and acceptance.

Men, it's okay to show your heart,
To be vulnerable, to share your fears,
It's not a sign of weakness,
But a sign of courage, dear brothers.
Your emotions are valid,
They deserve to be heard and seen,
Don't hide them or pretend,
Let your true self be seen.
Gentleness and care are beautiful traits,
Wear them on your sleeves with pride,
It doesn't diminish your masculinity,
It's a sign of the depth inside.
Speaking your truth is a brave act,
Opening up and being vulnerable,
It's a strength that deserves respect,
And admiration so incomparable.

I think most men desire to have a shoulder to lean on. Someone to talk to... Someone who'd listen without judgment. If only society didn't have the preconceived notion that men are supposed to be monuments of stoicism. Devoid of pain, anxiety, suffering, and depression. Believe it or not, we go through it. We are just good at hiding it. Because, tell me, what's the point of me opening up and sharing my troubles if society is going to look down on me and downplay my tribulations?

"Ink of Resilience"

My healing journey and the struggles I have faced and still face recovering from emotional and traumatic wounds. To forgive oneself and allow healing to take place is possible, but to recover from healed scars is another topic. I guess someday I'll be okay and find my footing in this dystopian world.

Finding out what works well for you when maneuvering mental health challenges comes down to understanding that there isn't a one-size-fits-all approach. Rather, it's about acknowledging where you are in your journey and exploring what resonates with your core. Always remember to take time and be mindful of yourself. Give yourself grace.

Some find solace in meditation,
Clearing their minds through contemplation.
Others find refuge in therapy,
Speaking their truth brings clarity.
Some seek comfort in medication,
Helping with depression's vexation.
Others turn to exercise and sweat,
A natural high to help forget.
Some find healing in community,
Sharing their struggles, gaining unity.
Others lean on friends and family,
Loved ones providing understanding, and empathy.
In the depths of your soul's unrest,
Know that support is never far away,
Embrace the solace that's best for you,
Hand in hand, we'll brave the stormy fray.

Hey there, just a gentle reminder that it's okay to:

● Not always feel comfortable with the people you love and surround yourself with

● Not have it together. Many of us are all trying to figure out our journey in life. Don't get pressured into thinking that you must have it all figured out by a certain age or within a certain timeline.

● Take breaks for yourself. Take time off to relax and enjoy the little things that life has to offer. Give your body and mind time to reboot.

● Feel angry at yourself. I beat myself up quite often. Also, the fact that I am an overthinker doesn't help. However, I don't dwell on it for too long.

● Feel tired. Listen, you aren't a robot. Make sure you get your beauty sleep. Don't forget to hydrate and eat your fruits.

You are seen, loved, and wanted.

It's 6:20 PM, and I'm alone in my apartment with the curtains shut, the lights off, and my phone set to airplane mode. I'm seated on my kitchen floor, and I'm trying so hard to search for a reason to keep on. However, what's keeping me from pulling the plug is the hope inside me that I choose to believe in.

I'm at a point where I'm just trying to keep it together to survive one day at a time. The end goal? Well, to see what amounts of my inconsolable existence if I hang onto dear life till my time comes.

The Art of Survival Down in The Dumps

I have a feeling this is not the end of the line for me. My time to depart has not yet come. I want to make the most of my life. I want to see what my life will amount to if I choose to stay the course and fight the good fight. I guess tonight I won't be crossing over to the other side.

Our mind is like a garden. We must tend to it regularly, pulling out the weeds of negative thoughts and watering the seeds of positivity, to help it flourish and grow.

Does it get better? Will I ever go back to being the old me? Well, I guess as the seasons draw to and end and time fades like sand in an hour glass, I'll know soon enough.

And suddenly, like an anchor lifted from a harbor, my problems felt lighter when I set foot into a bookstore... My solace and sweet escape from the constant darts of life constantly permeating my wheel of life and zeal to keep on living.

A river of thoughts flows through my mind,
Constantly churning, never left behind,
Anxiety, depression, and fear,
Each one trying to take the wheel and steer.
But I refuse to give in to their pull,
I'll take charge and find my peaceful lull,
Meditation is my steadfast guide,
A way to calm the stormy tide.
Sitting in silence, I breathe deeply,
Feeling a sense of calm seep,
Into every corner of my being,
A moment of solace, a moment of seeing.
Seeing through the veil of my thoughts,
Finding the clarity that I sought,
With every inhale and every exhale,
I release the tension, and let go of the tale.
That my mind tells me every day,
That I am not enough, that I should stray,
But in this moment of stillness, I know,
That I am enough, that I can grow.

Truly, battling and coping with mental health challenges can be an isolating and trying journey. However, it's essential to keep in mind that you aren't alone. Some people genuinely care about your well-being. Reach out to your loved ones because their words of encouragement and compassion can help you on your journey. Remember, you're loved, valuable, and cherished. Never forget!

In the stillness of my mind
I find a refuge, a tranquil space
A place where I can leave behind
The worries and the pain I face
Through meditation, I can cope
With the storm that rages inside
The anxiety, the fear, the hope
All the emotions I cannot hide
As I focus on my breath
I feel my body start to relax
My worries lose their hold on me
And I am free from their attacks
In this moment of serenity
I am empowered to face the day
My mind is clear, my soul is free
And I am ready to find my way

How I wish the moon would offer me its measly alms of light, just so I can fight my way through to the light of day, for I am at loggerheads with the darkness that threatens to devour me.

In the quiet breaths that fill my lungs,
I find solace that's often unsung.
For in the stillness of my mind,
I leave my worries far behind.
With every breath that I exhale,
I release the thoughts that make me pale.
The racing heart and troubled mind,
Are settled by this act divine.
As I sink into the silence deep,
My inner demons start to sleep.
For in this space of pure tranquility,
I find a strength that's born of humility.
With each passing moment, I feel at ease,
As I let go of all my worries and disease.
Meditation is my secret friend,
And on this path, I'll always depend.
When the weight of the world feels too much,
And your thoughts are a tangled rush,
Take a moment to breathe and just be,
Find stillness, and your spirit will fly free.

Lord knows how much I appreciate music artists, because on a day like today when my energy is low, I can plug in headsets, pump up the volume, and savor the melodies. Before I opted for music, I tried reading to distract myself because my thoughts tend to spiral out of control, and from time to time I'm compelled to tame the beast lest it drags me into a black hole, which often makes me use an astronomical amount of energy to pull myself out and get myself back together. Back to the music: today I'm soaking in *"Adagio for Strings."* What a perfect combination of dissonance, pace, and notes—a mere expression of what I'm feeling at the moment.

The devil is on my left shoulder, but the angel on the other whispers in a soft, subtle voice, *"Thread the needle and beat the devil."*

Self-care is not a luxury for the privileged but a necessity for everyone. It's all about taking responsibility for our own well-being and creating a foundation of resilience that can help us weather the storms of life.

There are days when my thoughts get the best of me and I forget to count my blessings, and like chaff in the wind, I wish I'd dissipate into nothingness. I don't care if God comes and takes me now.

There are days when I hear these noises, you know, these voices echoing loudly in my head, latching onto the cornerstone of my mind and following me everywhere.

I don't know your situation or what you've been through. My only hope is that my words will provide some sort of solace for your troubled soul. We may not be from the same continent or country, but like you, there are millions of us who are battling daily to stay sane in this cold, insane, and hellish world.

Separated by time and space but
united by pain.

Like a Salmon swimming upstream against the current, I'm also choosing to move forward despite the mental anguish and capitalist demands of the modern age because I have to see through my dreams and aspirations. Thus, I refuse to cave in and oblige to the misguided thoughts and demands that are currently wreaking havoc in my mind. I believe in myself; I'm more than a conqueror, and I'll weather this storm and ride the turbulent eddies of the tide.

In silence, I sit and ponder,
My thoughts like raging thunder,
Emotions gripping my very soul,
Mental health is a battle to console.
Tears stream down my weary face,
As I struggle to find my place,
Darkness clouds my every thought,
Banishing joy, leaving me distraught.

I've been through the grinder for the better part of my life, and sometimes I can't help but wonder whether there is a place for those like me in this pitiless world.

I hate my kind, which means I dislike myself. I wish I could be saved, but I'm far from saving. Even out in this foreign land where I escaped, life's good, yet it does nothing for me. It doesn't impress me. Well, at least I'm by myself, not ruining anyone's vibe by being silent or by talking. No one can reach me. Sigh, like it makes a difference anyway.
Mangled Thoughts

In my mind, there's always a storm
Thoughts and emotions take their form
Can't seem to shake this always-angry feeling
I can't ignore it or defend against it- it's revealing
But there's a way out of this maze
A silver lining to the darkest of days
Writing is my salvation, my shield
A safe space where I can truly yield
The pen in my hand flows and spills
My inner turmoil comes alive and chills
Ink and paper become my friend
As I see my burdens taking their end
Through writing, I find a calming breath
A way to navigate through the pain and death
It's not a complete resolution, but a start
To ease the weight and open my heart

Hi James,

I want you to know that I see you trying your best to piece together the pieces of your fragmented soul. I am proud of you because you have made it thus far. Keep going; you'll soon find yourself in the maze that you lost yourself in.

A Letter to Myself

I owe it to myself to create a different reality. Hopefully, this time it will be with a little less pain.

As someone who's manic-depressive. The lows hit you like Mike Tyson on the liver. And you're forced to crash and tumble. Topple that with my antisocial social behavior. It's the worst in the trenches... It sucks. Literally, because I'm alone and I want to scream for help, but there's no one to help me because all my life I've been a lone and pushed away everyone who has ever made an effort to draw closer to me. Yet I blame no one but myself.

In the depths of my mind, there lies
A battle I must face each day
A war between what's in my head
And what the world wants me to say
I find myself in a constant struggle,
With my thoughts that bring me pain,
Emotions crashing like a raging tide,
At times, impossible to explain.
But when I pick up my pen and write,
My feelings start to take flight,
Words become my shield and armor,
And I feel the weight begin to lighten.
Each line is like a healing balm
That soothes my soul and eases pain
It's like a window to my mind
That lets me see the storm and rain
Through writing, I find my way
Out of the darkness and into light
It's a journey that I must take
To make it through each endless night

Anything is possible; you can make a comeback and bounce back from any setback, provided you keep dancing to the rhythm of life.

"Threads of Connection"

This section dives into the impact of mental illness challenges on relationships. It explores the intricate dynamics between loved ones, offering insights into understanding, support, and the power of empathy in fostering healing and connection.

Without a doubt, mental health can become a challenge in relationships, and sometimes it might drive a wedge between the parties involved. However, let's all exercise empathy, tenderness, and unwavering support, because a problem half shared is half solved.

Mental illness can be a heavy load,
And relationships can feel corroded,
The burden is too much to bear,
And love can seem irreparable.
The highs and lows of manic depression,
Can make a relationship falter,
Depression's grip is hard to break,
And its effects, are hard to shake.
Anxiety can turn to fear,
And hopelessness is always near,
The stress of it all can take its toll,
And love can seem like a distant goal.
But with patience, care and understanding,
And support that is never demanding,
Love can conquer any trial,
And make it through the hardest mile.
Let us love with open hearts,
And see beyond the shattered parts,
Mental health challenges can't break,
The bonds that true love can create.

In each day's sun or storm
Lived two hearts, to each other sworn
In all joys and sorrows, they knew
A bond unbreakable and true
But as time passed, life took its toll
Challenges arrived, out of control
A storm brewed, from within one heart
Tears, anxiety, and sadness, torn apart
Mental health issues, unseen and strong
Distorting the thought process, all along
Innocent love turns into a battleground
For reasons unknown to the other, profound
The once-clear skies, now a misty path
Shrouded in darkness, a lover's wrath
Fears, paranoia, and insecurities dominate
Love, dwindling in a sea of hate

You'd be surprised by the number of people in the world who just crave to have someone who'd provide that comfortable silence. Someone who'd listen to their venting, their outbursts, and their overflow of thoughts and emotions without judgment, or someone who'd hug them and give them hope that it's going to be okay.

Only the Lord knows how long I have been trying to numb the pain, suffering, and frustrations of my mind by overworking and overdrinking, although it's safe to say that I have toned it down a notch in the drinking department.

Regardless, I know there are many like me who haven't been lucky enough to hear the right words that could uplift my spirit and sprinkle seeds of encouragement. But even then, just remember, even when you feel like this gloomy world has no place for you, you've got you, and God's got you.

Mental health challenges, they're not just in your head,
They can cause disruptions in your relationships instead.
Depression, anxiety, and everything in between,
Can leave you feeling lost, unsure and unseen.
Your partner may not understand what you're going through,
And that can lead to frustration and arguments too.
Communication is key, but sometimes it's hard,
To express your feelings when it feels like you're on guard.

It took me a while to understand that it's okay to ask others for help and to reach out in one's time of need. I don't know if anyone can relate, but I've always felt like I'd be bothersome if I asked people for help, so I always thug it out because that's the best way I know how. After all, I've always been at it alone, ever since I was a child. I have what we call a lone wolf persona. But like the adage says, "No man is an island," I came to terms with seeing it as normal to ask for help, for that's what friendship and brotherhood are for. I realized that by refusing to concede and ask for help, I was being selfish. Egotistical, if you will. Then again, life is a journey and a series of lessons. You always have to keep an open mind and be willing to learn and receive constructive criticism. That's how solid relationships and friendships are forged.

Mental health challenges can be tough,
They can disrupt and cause us to falter,
And in the realm of relationships,
Their impact can be felt like a thunderbolt.
A fleeting word that may have caused a smile,
Now results in a tear-filled mile,
The sweetness and joy that used to prevail,
Now replaced with a constant sense of betrayal.
Communication becomes a minefield,
Where words feed anger and not hope,
Demons come in at night to haunt,
And every thought feels like a slippery slope.
Loneliness lingers in the room,
Like a fog that refuses to lift,
Partners feel lost and helpless,
As they grapple with the difficult drift.
But amid the chaos and uncertainty,
The strength, love, and courage of the partners bloom,
A standing testament to the power of love,
And how it can shine through even the darkest gloom.
In the battle against mental ill-health,
Love becomes the glue that binds,
Through patience, compassion, and understanding,
The partners find peace and hope of a different kind.
And though the road is steep, and the journey long,
The power of love remains ever-strong,
For in the end, it is the love we share,
That gives us the courage to step out and dare.

I'll never forget. 15 October 2017. The youth service had ended, and we were out mingling. I remember this one girl, whom I later ended up dating, noticing that I was detached. I swear, I'll never forget her words. "I see you smiling and laughing, but your eyes tell a different story, one of sadness and melancholy. They're somber and subtly crying out for empathy. I couldn't believe it. It was like something straight out of a poetry book. To this day, she's one of the few people who have managed to see through my façade, and sometimes I can't help but wonder how many people can see the sadness through my eyes, even as I go about my life.

When mental health is not quite sound,
Friendship bonds can quickly unwind.
The challenges that come around,
Make it harder for us to align.
It's not just a simple bad day,
Anxiety, and depression take charge.
For friends, it's tricky to convey,
How much their support is larger.
The fear of judgment runs deep,
The stigma that carries in tow.
Overthinking before we speak,
Won't let our true feelings show.
Despite the hardships we face,
Friendship can still stand the test.
It takes a different kind of pace,
To reach out with care, as stressed.
When a friend is in distress,
Be the one who lends an ear,
Their inner turmoil, let it confess,
With friendship's touch, hold them dear.
In their fragile state of mind,
Embrace their struggles, don't let them hide,
For their mental well-being, be kind,
Let friendship's warmth forever abide.

I'm torn between having a social life or fleeing into reclusion from the obligation of socializing to just be solitary and alone. And if I'm being honest, every cell in my flesh painfully yearns for the latter.

Mental health challenges can at times make you feel like you're carrying the weight of the world alone, but it's essential to remember that you don't have to shoulder it alone. Share your burden with those you trust, and let them help you carry it. – I certainly wish I could take my advice. I'm used to carrying the weight of the world on my shoulders alone. It's been so for as long as trips down memory lane are concerned. Though I might mention it, just because I handle it well doesn't mean it doesn't wear me out. There are days when the load certainly feels a little heavier.

Friendship bonds are strong, or so we're often told
But mental health issues can make them grow cold
When worries and doubts take hold of the mind
It's easy to leave friends and support behind
We truly care and want to help ease your pain,
Yet, we do know not what more to do or say.
Our words may sound empty, and our efforts in vain,
When mental health troubles won't seem to sway.
We miss the old days when laughter ran free
When your mood didn't dictate all that, we'd be
But now we must walk on eggshells it seems
For fear of how we may set off extremes
We hope you know that we still care a lot
And we're here for when you want to talk or not
We know that life can be a battle sometimes
And we'll stand by you through those uphill climbs
When darkness descends and clouds your mind
Just know that your friends, we're never behind
We'll stay by your side through thick and thin
And help you find light from within.

I pray that you're the type of person who will hold down your spouse, friend, or boyfriend or girlfriend when they are going through a rough patch in their lives. Life has its ups and downs. I hope you won't be a deserter or runaway when the rubber meets the tarmac. Don't be the one that says, "I didn't sign up for this." Because if the tables were turned, I'm pretty sure you wouldn't want your close confidants to ghost you.

"Man-up" is often society's rebuttal to men who attempt to let the world know they are falling apart, and so in my bid to avoid being subjected to mockery, I suppressed my feelings and numbed my emotions. Still, I feel this fire burning in my soul; it's like a wildfire that runs ablaze, consuming everything in its path.

From a very tender age, I learned never to expect anything from anyone, not even friends. Because of my circumstances at the time, I had no choice but to mature fast, and I think to this day my lonesome approach to life has been reinforced to the point where I'll only reach out for help after I've tried everything in my power to find a solution but have come up short.

My world is imploding; I feel it weighing heavily on me, and in desperation, like a wildebeest gasping for air as it struggles to cross the Mara River, I let out a prayer: "God, don't let me fall. Your grace is needed; please keep me steadfast and stoic."

In darkness and doubt we find
Our loved ones lost and left behind
Their minds are a maze of broken thoughts
Their hearts weighed down by heavy knots
We see them struggle day by day
Invisible chains that make them fray
Their laughter once bright, now a memory lost
Their eyes a window, at such a cost
We try to help, to ease their pain
But sometimes our efforts seem in vain
Mental illness has a grip so tight
It dims the love that once shone brightly
We watch and wait, with hopes and fears
Sometimes we find ourselves in tears
For we love them still, with all our heart
Even when we are worlds apart
We won't give up, we won't retreat
For in each other, we find our heat
The fire that's fueled by love and care
And the courage to fight, every despair.

Strong, macho, and stoic men don't cry. Well, they do, but not in everyone's presence.

If you have reliable, trustworthy, and honorable friends you can fall back on when going through murky waters, lean on them. Just don't use them as emotional tampons because they can only do so much. If they're putting in 40% toward helping you get better, you've got to put in 60% or more. Remember, many of us have to walk through the wire before we can experience the delight of basking in stardust.

In the darkest of moments,
When the mind is a storm,
When the world feels too heavy,
And the heart is forlorn,
It's the love of a spouse,
That can bring back the light,
That can chase away shadows,
And make everything right.
When someone is hurting,
And their mind is in pain,
It's the touch of a hand,
That can soothe and sustain.
A listening ear,
And a heart that's open wide,
Can be a lifeline of hope,
For someone caught in the tide.

Please stop trying to hold me down, because I'm a broken soul, and what's the point of holding onto broken pieces if you'll only end up cut too? Why is it impossible for you to see that I'm sheltering you from misery?

Friends are treasures, kind and true,
Who offers support when we're feeling blue,
Through thick and thin, day by day,
They stick by us, showing us the way.
When the clouds of depression start to loom,
Our friends are there to light up the room,
They lend an ear and they lend a hand,
They make us feel like we can stand.
In moments of anxiety and despair,
Our friends remind us that they care,
They listen without judgment or blame,
And make us feel like we're not alone in the game.
It's the friends who offer a warm embrace,
And bring laughter to our tear-stained faces,
They lift us when we feel low,
And prove that love will always grow.
Cheers to the ones who stand by our side,
In the depths of the ever-darkening tide,
Their unwavering support, a precious gift,
Their understanding, a love that uplifts.
In their presence, we find solace and grace,
Their actions speak louder than words can trace,
Grateful are we for their unwavering care,
For their presence in our lives, is beyond compare.

You only need one to three solid friends who are in your corner and who are loyal, consistent, and honorable. Friends who won't abandon you in your time of need. Also, keep in mind that a genuine friendship dynamic doesn't require anything in return. True friendship is one where everyone views one another as equal and is devoid of competition. Consider yourself lucky if you have such a dynamic.

For a while, I tried to speak up and let my story be told, as the "boy child" has been encouraged to do in recent times, but the thing was, no one was willing to listen. So, can you really blame me for shutting the world out? And don't come around now, for I don't need your self-pity and sympathy. Where were you when I was drowning? This burden is mine to carry, and I shall shoulder it with dignity. So, please let me be, leave me to my own devices, and don't bother holding on to my memories; let them fade into oblivion.

Amidst desks and screens,
We find our daily routine.
Work and deadlines seem all,
As we try to meet our goals.
But amidst our busy lives,
We forget to take a pause,
To check on those who struggle,
With mental health and emotional flaws.
In a world that can be harsh,
A kind word can go miles,
To those who need it most,
It can bring back their smiles,
We should be the co-workers,
Who offer more than just work,
A listening ear and kind heart,
Can transform a life that's hurt.
Let's learn to be understanding,
And support each other in need,
Let's break the stigma around mental health,
And plant a seed of love and empathy.
For, in the end, it's our humanity,
That binds us all together,
Let's be there for each other,
In sunshine and stormy weather.
Let us pledge to be mindful,
Of those around us who may be struggling,
Let's offer help and support,
And be each other's haven.

When toiling away, stress and strain abound,
Overwhelming at times, tough to expound,
If mental health struggles come to light,
Co-workers offer a beacon of hope, shining bright.
Don't hesitate to speak up and share
About the challenges that you can't bear
Your colleagues may also have a story to tell
Together, you can create a supportive swell
Perhaps they'll take over some tasks
Or find ways to ease your mental asks
Maybe they'll just lend an ear
To listen, empathize and hear
Mental health is an important issue to address
One that we can't afford to suppress
So let your coworkers know they are not alone
Together, your workplace can become a mental health home.

The work environment can be quite toxic and can put a strain on one's mental health. Unproductive office politics, "witch hunting," and unhealthy competition are some of the notable factors that can cause mental fatigue in an office setting. Oh, how I wish everyone would get along seamlessly and respectfully. Wishful thinking, I suppose. Do your due diligence before signing that contract. Check out company reviews on websites like Glassdoor.

In the unfortunate event that you find yourself in a toxic work environment, leverage your leave days. Take time off to recoup and check on your mental health. Visit museums, attend musicals, and explore new books and music genres. In short, use this time to recuperate and do what sets your soul ablaze. If your situation becomes unbearable, you have the option of applying for another job opportunity. Hopefully, one with a healthy work environment that's drama-free and is not shackled to unnecessary office politics. All the best!

Dear Lord, why won't you lift this burden of overthinking, sadness, depression, and melancholy from me? I see what you do for others. I'm right here; sometimes I feel as though you're so close yet so far off. Why won't you help me? I am giving it my all. Literally, I'm hanging on by a thread, and it's taking my all just to stay afloat. Please don't abandon me. I don't want to have to say goodbye. Don't leave me in the cold. You're all I have left.

What deeper love compares to having a friend pray for you when you're going through a crisis? To have them mention your name when communicating with the Divine Deity, Lord of all creation. The fact that you're in their thoughts I mean, they are vouching for you. What an honor to be part of someone's most intimate moments when they're laying down not only their struggles but also your burdens before the Sole Creator of the universe. Certainly, their love for you must run deeper than the oceans.

The Purest form of love

Like a lone wolf in the blizzard, I was forced to survive, and now I can let out a silent sigh, knowing that once again I've lived to see the light of day. Oh, what joy it is to experience the warm embrace of the sun's rays shining down on me as if their sole intention was to catalyze and reignite my glimmering hope.

In the depths of darkness and despair,
When life seems too hard to bear,
It's family that can offer a light,
And make everything seem just right.
Their love so strong, their hearts so kind,
A haven for those in need to find,
A hand to hold, a shoulder to lean on,
When mental health battles can feel so long.
Through ups and downs, they stand beside us
With patience, empathy, and warmth inside,
Their unwavering support and understanding,
Is a healing balm for those who've been struggling.
Together they journey through the highs and lows,
With each step forward, the love further grows,
Family is the anchor that keeps us grounded,
A helping hand that's always found it.
In the depths of mental strain,
Remember, dear one, you're not alone,
Within your family's embrace, lies a gain,
Love, support, understanding clearly shown.
Their hearts, a sanctuary of solace,
A refuge from the storms you face,
Together, forever, they'll hold you close,
A haven of care, a sacred space.

I yearn to be understood, for acceptance, for love, for a hug, but of all these scars I've garnered, who will be accepting and receptive of me now?

For all those I have shunned, pushed, and cast away. I am sorry. I need to be alone for some time. I know it causes you great anguish, but at the moment I need to be selfish, for I am drowning at sea and I need to relearn how to come afloat once again. Give me time and space. If the good Lord wills, we'll definitely cross paths again. However, for now, I must tread this path alone.

"Beneath The Surface"

Centered on healing and recovery, this section explores the resilience of the human spirit. The messages here illuminate the journey of growth, acknowledging the small victories, moments of joy, and the ups and downs when you are trying to rebuild a meaningful life after weathering the storms of life.

Curled into a fetal position, I lay, tears streaming down my glowered face, wondering whether I'd ever be whole again. Whether I'll heal from what afflicts and torments my peace of mind, yet despite giving it my all, I always wind up right where I started—alone, filled with razor-sharp pain, empiteness, and thoughts running wild like Mustangs in the mountains. (Exhales), I am mentally and emotionally downcast.

Some days would dawn, and I'd not bother drawing the curtains. The darkness, pin-drop silence, and my bed (talk about going through the escapades of manic depression). Yet, I wouldn't try to escape this moment; I'd choose to wholly embrace it in its entirety, knowing well that it was just one of those days, you know, where my mind would choose to remind me of my dreary existence.

In the depths of our minds,
Lies a world we cannot see,
Where monsters and demons roam,
Threatening our sanity.
But there is a light that shines,
A beacon of hope and grace,
Through the darkness it guides,
Our minds to a better place.

There are days I hit the sack but can't sleep because my brain won't shut down. Thoughts, sad memories of past experiences, anxiety, and worry are all top contenders for my insomnia. Likewise, there are days when I feel the weight of the world on my shoulders and am unmotivated to see the day through, mostly due to my anxiety, wondering when it'll ever end. But on such days, I've always remembered to ask my Creator for help for his grace, which is sufficient.

I don't know what you may be going through in your life—the battles you're fighting, the pain and suffering you are enduring. I'm not going to sit here and say that I understand how you feel or what you are going through, because everyone's circumstances are different.

But I pray for everyone who's reading this and going through a rough patch in their life. May God grant you the grace to see it through. I pray you won't throw in the towel. Admittedly, sometimes the thought of despair crosses my mind, though I always remind myself that I've got to keep on living, even though it sometimes kills me inside. I've got to see it through. What if it all works out in the end? I've realized pain is inevitable in this life, and things don't always work out as we'd expect. Maybe we've got to suffer a bit before it all comes together. Beloved, we have to keep pushing regardless. It'll be okay, alright? This, too, shall pass. Keep fighting the good fight; I'm rooting for you!

In the darkness of the mind,
Where pain and shadows intertwine,
There is a glimmer of hope,
A spark that shines divine.
With every word and verse, we write,
We pave a path to healing and light,
Through the beauty of language,
And the power it ignites.
The struggles we face,
In a mind that's bruised and displaced,
Find comfort and ease,
In the books & poetry, we embrace.
Through verse and rhyme,
We discover solace and grace in due time,
As we venture towards,
A brighter, happier climb.
Let your words spill out,
From deep within, without a doubt,
And explore the depths,
Of your innermost devout.
For with a steadfast heart,
And words that flow with ease and craft,
We can conquer all,
And rise anew at last.

Dear God Almighty, I pray to you every other day, waiting patiently and hopefully for some of your help. Would you please help me, oh gracious savior? Out of the kindness of your heart, please shine your face on me, for my might and will are fading off like the light of day into the darkness. Don't distance yourself from me, alone in this world; you're all I have left. Oh, Savior, don't forsake me in this glum world. Please help me.

I pray God heals you from the things you don't talk to anyone about.

Amidst the depths of despair,
Where hopelessness looms supreme,
Stands a shadowed figure all alone,
Lost in a broken dream.
Tattered and torn, they're falling apart,
Wounded in ways no one can see,
The weight of the world crushing their heart,
Emotions are unable to break free.
Their mind is a battlefield, a warzone,
Every breath is a fight to survive,
Relentlessly they strive for a place to call theirs,
To banish the fear and stay alive.
But hope still shines, a flicker of light,
Breaking through the darkness within,
A spark of strength to ignite,
And start the journey to begin.
Each step is a victory, each day a fight,
One foot in front of another,
The road ahead may be dark as night,
But the journey brings us closer.
Closer to the person we were before,
To the life, we thought we'd lost.

At some point, you'll realize you no longer shed tears in the face of adversity. That's because you've grown stronger. It reminds me of how diamonds are formed under excessive pressure and intense conditions, which is why, to date, they're the hardest metal ever known to humanity. Give yourself a pat on the back because, like a phoenix, you've risen from the ashes. You've broken the chains of whatever was afflicting you and holding you back.

Sometimes I appreciate the fact that I have to wear prescribed photochromic glasses. I can't begin to imagine the few inquisitive souls that have the gift of peering through one's eyes and seeing into one's soul. But maybe all I want is to be drawn out, for someone to look through the sadness harbored in my eyes and usher some tenderness into my soul.

The cost of healing, the cost of change,
The cost of facing our fears,
The cost of shedding our old skin,
And conquering our tears.
But the price is worth the reward,
To find the peace that we deserve,
To walk a path once ignored,
And learn to love and to serve.
Take heart, dear soul,
Your journey has just begun,
And though the road may be hard to stroll,
Know that you are not alone.

Being someone who hardly shares the intricate details of what's going on, sometimes my problems tend to get the best of me. In these trying moments, I forget about counting my blessings and wish God would call me home.

I awakened in the morning in high spirits, and I hit the sack devoid of dark, pensive, and gloomy thoughts. A remarkable improvement, I suppose, given the internal woes I have had to contend with.

When you're fighting anxiety and depression. You're like the walking dead. A lifeless being that hangs on by a thread to the essence of life—in a nutshell, add lifelessness and overthinking to the mix, and you've got yourself a potent concoction of despair. It sucks! It's like having a leech on your body; the difference is that this time, instead of sucking blood, it's sucking your life force.

The Darkness that Lingers

The night is long and lonely,
and in the silence, I hear
the echoes of my darkest fears,
the whispers of my deepest sorrows.
But in the morning light,
I rise tall and strong,
my spirit shining bright,
my heart singing a new song.
The journey to healing is long and hard,
with twists and turns and hills to climb,
but with each step, I find my way,
leaving the past behind.
There are days when I stumble,
when the darkness creeps in,
but I know I'm not alone,
I have the strength within.
I keep on walking,
with hope burning in my heart,
knowing that each day is a new chance
to make a brand-new start.
And though the road may be rocky,
and the journey may be long,
I will keep on walking,
and my spirit will keep on strong.
For I have tasted the sweetness of life,
and I know that I can rise above
the pain and the sorrow,
and soar on wings of love.

At first, you'll shed plenty of tears and spend endless nights asking the universe why you can't seem to grab a hold of happiness. It'll be one of the darkest phases of your life, but don't worry because the tears are like an outlet for the pain, sorrow, and melancholy in your heart. There are days you'll cry yourself to sleep, and those are some of the days that you'll experience some of the best sleep. It takes time, but soon you'll shed no more tears. You are going to be alright, okay? It's a bad phase, not a bad life. I'm rooting for you, and I can't wait for you to bounce back.

Yours Truly

The sound of my ringtone is unfamiliar. Common voices of those I talked to often, slowly fading into the now distant mirage... I then reside to myself, alone with my burdens, anguished mind, and downtrodden heart.

While I tread along the winding road,
My mental health takes on a heavy load,
But through the trials and the pain,
I know that I can heal again.
My mind may falter, my thoughts may spin,
But with patience and love, I can begin,
To find my strength, my inner peace,
And let the healing process increase.
I'll take each step with a hopeful heart,
And keep moving forward from the start,
Through therapy, meditation, and rest,
I'll restore my mind and be at my best.
And though the path may be long,
I know that I can be strong,
For healing is a journey to embark on,
I'm determined to make my mark.
Let the sun shine through the clouds,
As I discover the strength that lies within,
With each day, my heart will heal and grow,
And my mind will be free to explore and know.

How nice it would be to have someone who would facilitate my healing journey! To show me how to heal these wounds and the bitterness and trauma that I have experienced during the course of my life. Because, whether I'd like to admit it or not, they have placed an unprecedented weight on my soul. Despite it all, I am learning to let go and let God's peace reign supreme. I can't say I am there yet. Similarly, I am imperfect, but I am learning to take the leap of faith and cast away all that troubles my heart, for I wish to live and not just exist.

Overcoming mental health is not just about finding happiness but also about finding a sense of purpose and meaning in life. I, for one, have come to terms with the fact that lasting happiness comes from living your purpose. Vanity can only make you happy for so long.

Amidst the chaos of your mind,
A light flickers, hard to find.
But hold on tight, don't let it fade,
For within you, a warrior is made.
The journey to healing is never easy,
But trust the path, it'll leave you breezy.
One step at a time, you'll be sure to find your way,
And the sun will shine bright on a new day.
It's okay to reach out for a helping hand,
To carve a new life, one that's grand.
Surround yourself with love and care,
And soon enough, you'll find yourself.
The scars may seem deep, and the pain immense,
But you'll rise above it all, with a gentle touch.
Your heart will soar with newfound hope,
And from the darkness, you'll learn to cope.
The process of healing is not linear,
But with each fall, you'll grow stronger.
Rise, dear one, and claim your victory,
For inside you lies a mighty legacy.
Always remember, you aren't alone,
And your struggle is not a burden to atone.
With love, perseverance, and grace,
You'll take back your power, and flourish at your own pace.

Your exhaustion is not shameful. You are not a failure because you are mentally, physically, spiritually, or emotionally tired. It's okay to feel overwhelmed. You're not less human just because it's difficult for you to keep up with the capitalistic demands and pace of this new era.

I had been locked out of heaven and all its glory divine for what seemed like an eternity, my existence doomed to the sunken abysmal hopelessness of the darkness, and yet I somehow escaped the Devil's Triangle, but not bereft of the scars of war that have left a healed laceration in my soul, and sometimes I feel as though someone has run a blunt Santoku knife through it, and it tends to hurt, and I scream loudly with my lips clumped, "Take it easy! Take it easy! Take it easy, James!"

Chronicles of a rattled mind

Amid turmoil and strife
There are small moments that brighten life
A smile from a friend or a sunny day
Can brighten the gloom and make way
For progress and healing to take place
Bringing a smile to your face
These moments of joy, however small
Can help you take down the walls
That keeps you from moving forward
And make your progress much slower
With each moment of happiness and peace
You'll find your struggles start to decrease

It's been a while since I smiled and felt genuine happiness and joy bubbling within me. I'm not sad or anything, that's for sure. I guess there are just moments when I feel a bit numb. It took me a while to start finding joy and happiness in the simple things because, for the longest time, I thought of happiness as nothing but a pipe dream, a fleeting emotion.

To me, happiness and joy look like:

- When someone notices intricate details about myself, especially if I hadn't noticed them myself,

-Reading books while drinking black coffee and eating my scrambled puffed eggs.

-Rain just before I hit the sack.

-The smell of paper on old paperback books

-The sound of the ocean waves colliding

-Poems that resonate with every fiber of my body.

-Writing

- Listening to the latest EDM releases from the *"This Never Happened YouTube channel"*

In moments of despair and pain,
When darkness seemed to reign,
There came a shining light,
A promise of a better fight.
From deep within, a spark was born,
A flicker of hope that shone,
With grit and strength, a journey began,
To heal and grow, to rise again.
Through valleys low and peaks so high,
You journeyed on, you did not lie,
With each step taken, a victory is won,
A new day dawned a brighter sun.
The moments of joy, progress, born,
In every little step, a heart is reborn,
A new you arises, gentle and strong,
Wings unfurled, a melody of a song.
And as you soar, higher and higher,
Unafraid of what may transpire,
Know that your courage carries far,
A beacon of hope, a guiding star.
For in moments of pain and strife,
You found the strength to change your life,
And in that journey, you did unfold,
A heart of gold, a story told.

Hopefully, I'll be alright. It's just one of those days, right? I want the old me. I mean, I miss the old me. Life used to be so nice. I never used to feel this way. Does it really get better?

I suffer alone in silence, and I torment myself to the brink of destruction. I'm on the edge, and I could willingly answer the call of the void. And what's with this sunken, depthless feeling in my chest? I'm starting to feel as though this journey is too much for me.

l'appel du vide

I look great on the outside, but deep down, I'm not doing well. I'm also not the happiest person, but no one can tell because I am an excellent actor, and I never seek out help because I'd rather get through it myself. My overthinking makes me think that asking others for help or a listening ear is a burden. I mean, they already have their battles to contend with, right?

A glimmer of hope, with each step forward,
A newfound strength that helps us cope,
The moments of joy and progress,
When mental health challenges we address.
The pain may linger, but so does the light,
The promise of a better tomorrow, not out of sight,
For every hurdle we overcome,
A sense of pride, a beating of the drum.
We celebrate each milestone, big or small,
For they represent strength and courage overall,
During darkness, we find our way,
And gradually, the light leads us to a new day.
Embrace the moments of joy and progress,
For they remind us, we can overcome any stress,
Healing and recovery is a journey, not a race,
And with each victory, we find peace and grace.

There are days when you'll feel a gravitational pull back into the blackness, the deep, dark depths of the abyss. On these days when you feel like you are drowning, may you master the courage and strength to remain afloat and keep your head above the water. As long as you pull through, that's what I look forward to.

In the darkness of my mind,
I struggled to leave it all behind,
Manic depression held me tight,
Yet I fought with all my might.
Days felt impossible,
Trapped in a world inescapable,
But hope shone through,
As I started something new.
When darkness creeps in at night,
I choose to let the joy ignite,
Remembering every triumph,
In my heart, forever triumphant.

Try just a little bit harder. Try just a little bit more. I know the journey toward healing and self-discovery hasn't been easy. But I don't know if you realize how far you've come. Yes, you may not be there just yet, but it's too late to look back now. Don't be like Lot's wife from the Bible, who looked back and got turned into salt. Focus on the path and steps ahead of you. You've got this, and if no one's rooting for you, I am, and I can't wait to see you overcome all that torments and wears down your mind.

In moments of struggle and strife,
When shadows engulf our weary days,
It's easy to lose sight of life,
And stumble through the maze of disarray.
But when the clouds begin to part,
And the rays of hope breakthrough,
There's a glimmer in the heart,
A sense of progress made anew.
Small steps forward, each one savored,
As we find our strength and our voice,
We learn to heal, our fears unshackled,
And we grow, for we have a choice.
With each victory, big or small,
We find ourselves steadier and surer,
As we rise from our crawl,
And learn to live and to endure.
And as we journey on this road,
Full of twists and turns and bends,
We'll find our strength and our abode,
With each step that we transcend.
Let's revel in the bliss,
This fleeting moment of growth,
For we've mastered the art,
Of mending our wounded souls.

If it's possible, invest in some quality headsets or wireless earpieces and drown yourself in high-vibrational music. It has a way of calming the soul and slowing down a racing mind. To this day, I always have my air pods with me. Certainly, it's become an essential part of my life. Without them, I feel naked. You can always try and see if the same approach will yield positive results in your life.

I've learned to forgive myself and everyone else before I go to sleep at night, and I've realized healing happens more rapidly when I do.

From the depths of darkness and despair
Where hope seemed like a distant dream,
We found the strength to rise and overcome,
To mend and fix our minds with a steady stream.
For progress is a gift that brings new life,
A beacon of hope in a world of strife,
As we continue our journey forward,
We know that healing is the reward.

Nature has such a profound healing effect. Just being out in the wild, soaking in the fresh natural breeze while listening to the birds chirp, is like a dream come true. Plus, how can I forget the profound feeling of my demons letting go?

When darkness descends
And your mind becomes a maze
Where hope and light seem lost
And you're trapped in a daze
Fear not, dearly beloved
For you are not alone
You have the strength within
To make the darkness known
The road may be steep
With twists and turns galore
But with each step
You'll overcome it all
The clouds will clear away
And sunshine will soon break
The happiness you seek
Will come with each stride you take
Lift your head high
And let your spirit soar
For you have overcome
What you thought was your downfall

What do you see when you stare into your own eyes in the mirror? I see a doorway that ushers me into a labyrinth of pent-up pain, suffering, and unhealed wounds. Sigh, I've got a lot of healing to do.

Sometimes happiness can seem like an elusive dream. The more you aspire to attain it, the more it escapes your grasp. Notwithstanding, I think you can have a shot at a life of happiness if you learn to forgive yourself and others. Let go of grudges; they'll weigh you down. Allow yourself to grow into your higher self and experience the goodness of life.

"Breaking The Chains"

Addressing the stigma and discrimination that surround mental health, in this section I shine a light on the importance of awareness and understanding. The poems, thoughts, and messages advocate for a society that embraces mental health as an essential part of the human experience, fostering compassion, empathy, and support.

Mental illness is not a choice, but stigma is. Let's choose kindness, empathy, and understanding instead of judgment and discrimination.

Mental health, so often ignored,
Stigma and discrimination still abound.
It's time for us to become informed,
And show compassion all around.
Challenges are faced by those with issues,
Their battles are fought both inside and out.
You never know the pain they go through,
Let us end prejudice, without a doubt.
We all agree It's time for a change, and
Mental health should be discussed with ease.
Empathy and kindness are what we need to see,
And not the judgment that causes unease.
Everyone has their story to tell,
Not everyone's struggles are visible as well.
Let's take a step toward being well,
And change our ways for mental health's sake to dwell.
We'll start today, with hearts full of care,
And promise ourselves to be more aware.
Let's embrace all, be kind and fair,
Together we'll create a delightful world.

It's okay to cry. No one should shame you for shedding tears because of your melancholy. If anything, I think tears are the outlet of pain, helping to decompress the burdens of one's heart. Like an ostrich that burrows its head in the sand, I too have burrowed my head in hiding into my pillow and wept to my heart's content.

In the silence of the mind,
There lies a truth hard to find,
A truth that few can understand,
The struggle of a tormented mind.
We often close our eyes and ears,
To the plight of those living in fear,
But words can be a powerful ally,
In changing the world and breaking the lie.
Let us speak of mental health,
And the struggles that come with it,
Let us address the stigma and discrimination,
And work to lift the veil bit by bit.
For a person's worth is not defined,
By their struggles or state of mind,
A heart that's kind and a true soul,
Is all that matters, through and through.
Let's all embrace the power of words,
And use them to change the world,
To create a world of empathy and love,
Where each soul can be unfurled.

There's a stigma around mental health,
that keeps so many in stealth,
afraid to seek help or speak out,
leaving them in pain and doubt.
Discrimination only adds to the pain,
making it harder to break the chain,
of shame and fear that weigh them down,
turning their smiles into frowns.
It's time to put an end to the shame and stigma,
and treat mental health just the same,
as we do any other medical issue,
without judgment or seeking refuge.
Let's open up and lend a hand,
and help those who can't withstand,
the burdens of mental health they face,
and ensure they have a better place.
We're all human, and we all must cope,
with the ups and downs that life may hope,
let's all be kind and compassionate,
and break the stigma, it's never too late.

The shame and stigma surrounding mental health prevent so many people from seeking help and living their best lives. It's time to see mental health as just as important as physical health and treat it with the same level of care and respect.

I feel robbed of my elixir of life. You invaded my mind, consumed whatever shred of joy and happiness I had left, and left me an empty shell. You've forced me to become an actor, to the point where I have to act like I am this happy soul. But it's too late now; the pretense continues and the façade prevails. You've molded me into this... Sigh, I'm beat. If only I could hug myself.

Invisible pains within the mind,
Buried deep where most won't find,
A struggling soul in constant fight,
But to the world, everything's all right.
Stigma and fear still exist,
Around these struggles that persist,
As flawed judgments seek to contain,
Limit and confine those in pain.
We must seek to understand,
The struggles of our fellow man,
To open up our hearts and minds,
And leave prejudice far behind.
For these wounded souls, let's be kind,
Honor their battles and help them find,
Hope and healing for their strife,
And end the stigma that taints their life.
Let's speak up, let's take a stand,
Let's lend a helping, loving hand,
Let's break through barriers that oppress,
And heal the broken, hurt, and distressed.
For, in the end, we are all one,
Our struggles are shared under the same sun,
And together we can rise above,
To build a world of empathy and love.

When life backs you up against the wall, you often find yourself sinking into the cold, deep, and darkest depths of the ocean, where it's hard to breathe, let alone ask for help.

In silence, our minds twist and turn,
Caught in shadows of unknown concern.
The stigma of mental health it seems,
A weighty burden that tears at our seams.
But words, oh words can break these chains,
The power of prose to ease our pains.
Poems that speak to our innermost core,
Shining light on what we can't ignore.
The voices that rise from deep within,
Echo a struggle we need not contain.
For in the darkness, we are not alone,
On the page, we find a loving home.
So let us break this taboo at last,
And bring our pain into the light so vast.
May our words be a balm to those who ache,
And our poems the beacon for those who wait.

Discrimination against those with mental illness only perpetuates the cycle of suffering and silence. Let's break the cycle and create a world where everyone feels safe and supported to talk openly about their mental health.

It soon dawned on me that this world was a cruel place that offered no solace to those with sadness in their hearts.

Even after I had no more tears to shed, I always wondered whether this life was worth living. I pondered on it long enough, and I arrived at the conclusion that perhaps I could help others gracefully bear the burdens of this world through my words. After years of constantly journaling my thoughts and writing poetry, I have chosen to let the world in. Hopefully, my experiences and words will help you navigate your journey as you try to figure out the game of life. And yes, life is worth living; you just have to find your reason, and believe me, if you search within long enough, you too will find a reason to live. Frankly, there's nothing quite as fulfilling.

Words are formidable. They can make or break a person, and so we're called upon to be mindful. You don't know what people are going through or the demons they have to contend with daily. They might be on their last straw, and your unkind and unsavory words are what push them over the edge. Be a voice of healing.

Within our minds and hearts,
We are all a work of art.
But when the clouds begin to gather,
And our thoughts begin to tether,
It seems the world begins to falter.
We're told to keep our minds in check,
To keep our feelings in a fleck,
And to never let them see us as weak,
Or we'll be labeled as a freak.

People struggling with mental illness
Often feel they go at it alone
Let's work together, do our part
To create a kinder tone
Let's spread awareness, educate
And break down the stigma wall
So those who suffer every day
Don't feel so small
Let's listen to their stories
And try to understand
The weight they carry every day
And lend a helping hand
We all have the power to make a difference
To help our fellow man
Let's show empathy and compassion
And help heal the pain of the mind's strain
To those fighting mental health
Know that you are not alone
We stand with you, hand in hand
Together we'll make a home.

It's sad how some people can mock and belittle those going through anxiety and depression when they haven't walked a mile in their shoes. Either way, you've got this. Trust yourself when you haven't a clue what's next and have hit rock bottom. I want you to know that you are capable of making lemonade when life gives you lemons.

Don't mock a pain you haven't endured

Amidst the chaos of our daily lives,
A silent struggle goes unnoticed.
A heart, once filled with joy and light,
Now cloudy, dark, and hopelessly bleak.
Mental torment, a burden hard to bear,
Isolation is a feeling hard to share.
A soul that longs for peace and care,
Yearns for acceptance, a rare love.
The world's quick to judge and dismiss,
The pain that lies behind the mask.
Unseen, and unheard, the agony persists,
A silent demon that's hard to unmask.

All I know is that it hurt a lot, but crying helped. Such dark days those were; I'm glad they are behind me. But imagine that not a single soul knew. I must have hidden my pain well, for I didn't want to impose it on anyone. My mental challenges and creeping depression were my burdens to carry. One thing is certain: My mother's prayers kept me going in my darkest days, when I couldn't find my way.

"La Fin"

I'm glad you made it this far. Mine is just to thank you for taking time to read through my personal journey ever since I began documenting and journaling it down in early 2017. Much of what I have written down in this book has been unknown to many, especially those closest to me. The last few years have not been a walk in the park, and every day I have had to strive to find a reason to push on. All I can say is that it gets better with time. Although there are days when the darkness seems to wrap its arms around me, finding the lighthouse sometimes seems burdensome. Regardless, what matters is that I'm still here. I haven't given up on myself, and neither should you.

Feel free to say hello on *Instagram*. **@_jamesb_writes**

Until next time, that's all for now. Keep well, and may the God of Abraham preserve you.

About the Author

Born and raised in Nairobi, Kenya, James B. Agape discovered solace in writing back in 2017, using it as an outlet to cope with life's challenges. However, it wasn't until recently that he decided to share his introspective musings, messages, and poetry with the world.

His debut collection, "Pent Up Thoughts," delves into the themes of anxiety, depression, self-love, healing, and the stigma surrounding mental illness—issues he has personally grappled with throughout much of his adult life.

James firmly believes that writing and self-expression require no formal qualifications; all it takes is a genuine desire to welcome readers into one's world through the power of words.